A GARDEN *of* IMPRESSIONIST VERSE

NINETEENTH–CENTURY FRENCH POETRY

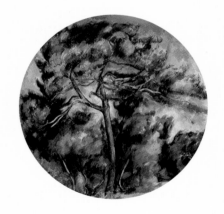

F

FRANCES LINCOLN LIMITED

PUBLISHERS

CONTENTS

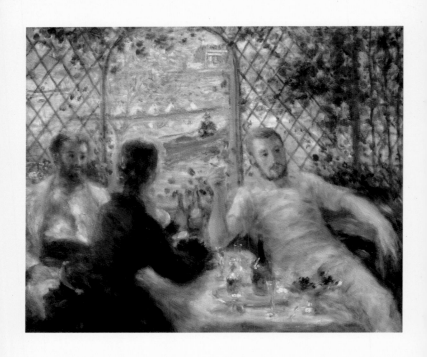

Il pleut, il pleut enfin!
  Et la vigne altérée
  Va se voir restaurée
Par ce bienfait divin.
  De l'eau chantons la gloire,
  On la méprise en vain,
C'est l'eau qui nous fait boire
  Du vin! du vin! du vin!

Mais à vous chanter l'eau
  Je sens que je m'altère
  Donnez mois vite un verre
Du doux jus du tonneau —
Ce vin vient de la Loire,
  Ou bien des bords du Rhin;
C'est l'eau qui nous fait boire
  Du vin! du vin! du vin!

PRAISE OF WATER

The rain, the rain at length;
And from the gift divine
The parched and drooping vine
Recovers life and strength.
The praise of water sing,
Let none the theme decline;
Since doth from water spring
Wine! wine! refreshing wine!

While water's praise I sound,
I feel my throat grow dry;
Quick, push the bottle round,
Which doth the flask supply.
And merry friends, I think,
If you my chorus join,
Water will make you drink
Wine, wine, exulting wine!

Armand Gouffé, 'Eloge de l'eau',
tr. H. Carrington

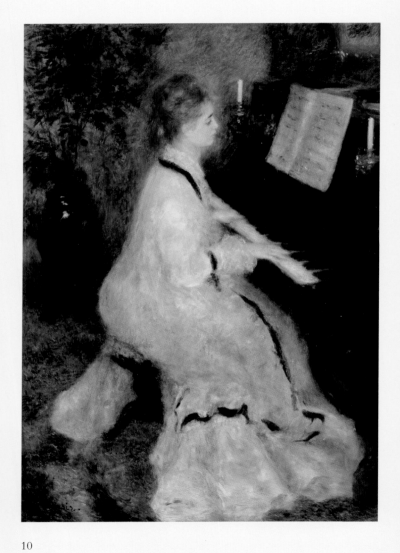

THE PIANO

The keyboard, over which two slim hands float,
Shines vaguely in the twilight pink and grey,
Whilst with a sound like wings, note after note
Takes flight to form a pensive little lay
That strays, discreet and charming, faint, remote,
About the room where perfumes of Her stray.

Paul Verlaine, 'Ariettes oubliées',
from Romances sans paroles
(1874), tr. anon.

Le piano que baise une main frêle
Luit dans le soir rose et gris vaguement,
Tandis qu'avec un très léger bruit d'aile
Un air bien vieux, bien faible et bien charmant
Rôde discret, épeuré quasiment,
Par le boudoir longtemps parfumé d'Elle.

INVITATION TO THE VOYAGE

My child, my sister,
Think of the sweetness
Of going there to live together!
To love at leisure,
To love and to die
In a country that is the image of you!
The misty suns
Of those changeable skies
Have for me the same
Mysterious charm
As your fickle eyes
Shining through their tears.

There, all is harmony and beauty,
Luxury, calm and delight.

Charles Baudelaire, 'L'Invitation au voyage'
from Les Fleurs du Mal
(1857), tr. A. Symons

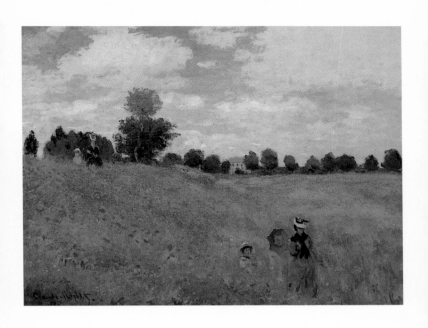

Mon enfant, ma sœur,
Songe à la douceur
D'aller là-bas vivre ensemble!
Aimer à loisir,
Aimer et mourir
Au pays qui te ressemble!
Les soleils mouillés
De ces ciels brouillés
Pour mon esprit ont les charmes
Si mystérieux
De tes traîtres yeux,
Brillant à travers leurs larmes.

Là, tout n'est qu'ordre et beauté,
Luxe, calme et volupté.

THREE GOLDEN THREADS

Like a swallow I'd fly and leave my love
  Forgotten beyond the sea;
But with cruel threads that are garden–wove
  She holdeth the heart of me.

One is her look and two her smile
  And three is her mouth so red;
And I dare not strain for a single mile
  Or tighten her threefold thread.

I would I might break their bonds and fly,
  And so with my grief have done.
Ah, no! for these three I would sooner die
  Than sever a single one!

Charles-Marie-René Leconte de Lisle,
'Tre Fila d'Oro', from Poésies complètes
(1858), tr. W. Thorley

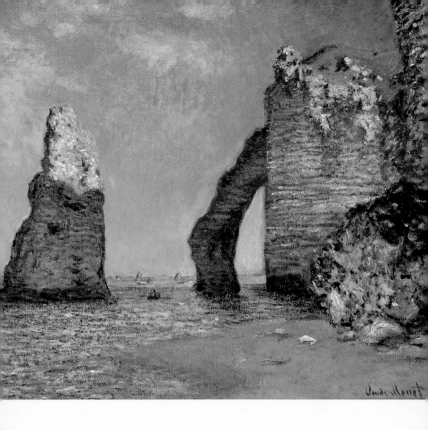

Là-bas, sur la mer, comme l'hirondelle,
Je voudrais m'enfuir, et plus loin encore!
Mais j'ai beau vouloir, puisque la cruelle
A lié mon cœur avec trois fils d'or.

L'un est son regard, l'autre son sourire,
Le troisième, enfin, est sa lèvre en fleur;
Mais je l'aime trop, c'est un vrai martyre:
Avec trois fils d'or ella pris mon cœur!

Oh, si je pouvais dénouer ma chaîne!
Adieu, pleurs, tourments; je prendrais l'essor.
Mais non, non! mieux vaut mourir à la peine
Que de vous briser, ô mes trois fils d'or!

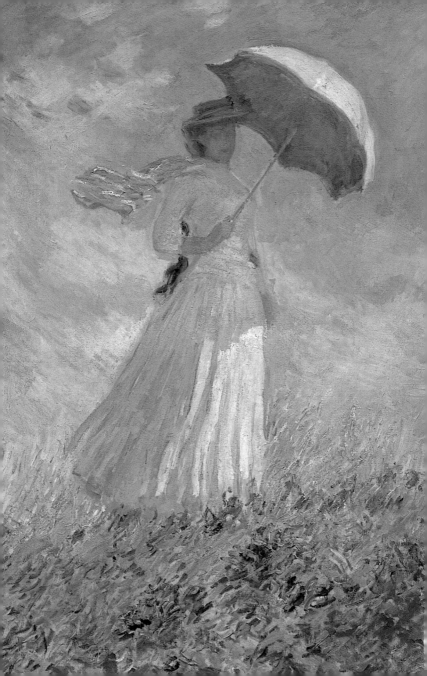

WINGS OF LOVE

My verse should alight, O Love,
   Within your garden, if my words
But beat the same soft wings above
   As bear aloft the birds.

Like wafted sparks, my words adrift
   Should fill your hearth, a glowing throng,
If they but bore the wings that lift
   This loving heart in song.

They'd flock to you by night and day,
   Still staunch in their sweet tarryings,
If but my verses beat a way
   With Love's unwearied wings.

Victor Hugo, from Les Contemplations
(1856), tr. W. Thorley

Mes vers fuiraient, doux et frêles,
Vers votre jardin si beau,
Si mes vers avaient des ailes,
Des ailes comme l'oiseau.

Ils voleraient, étincelles,
Vers votre foyer qui rit,
Si mes vers avaient des ailes,
Des ailes comme l'esprit.

Près de vous, purs et fidèles,
Ils accourraient nuit et jour,
Si mes vers avaient des ailes,
Des ailes comme l'amour

CORRESPONDANCES

In Nature's shrine confusèd speech doth stir
  Among her vibrant columns, man doth tread
  Where forests of strange symbols still unread
With their bland looks behold the wayfarer.
As moaning echoes that in distance blur
  And in wide aisles of cloudy rumour wed,
  So, vast as darkness or as light, is spread
The speech whereby scent, sound, and hue confer.

Some scents are chill and infants' flesh, a draft
  Breathed on an oboe, green of a green blade;
Others will in their reeky triumph waft
  A wind from unimaginable poles;
  Musk, benzoin, ambergris, by each is made
  The song of the loud rapture of men's souls.

Charles Baudelaire, 'Correspondances'
from Les Fleurs du Mal *(1857), tr. W. Thorley*

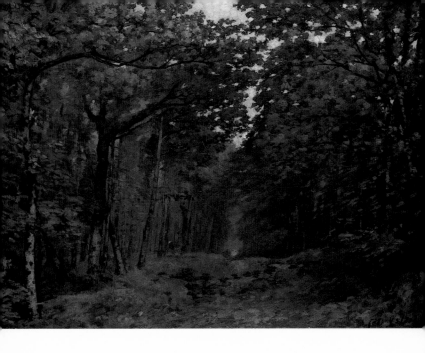

La nature est un temple où de vivants pilier
Laissent parfois sortir de confuses paroles;
L'homme y passe à travers des forêts de symboles
Qui l'observent avec des regards familiers.

Comme de longs échos qui de loin se confondent
Dans une ténébreuse et profonde unité,
Vaste comme la nuit et comme la clarté,
Les parfums, les couleurs et les sons se répondent.

Il est des parfums frais comme des chairs d'enfants,
Doux comme les hautbois, verts comme les prairies,
– Et d'autres, corrompus, riches et triomphants,

Ayant l'expansion des choses infinies,
Commes l'ambre, le musc, le benjoin et l'encens,
Qui chantent les transports de l'esprit et de sens.

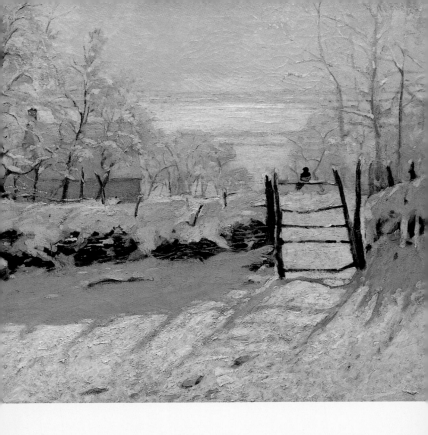

Qu'il est doux, qu'il est doux d'écouter des histoires,
Des histoires du temps passé,
Quand les branches d'arbres sont noires,
Quand la neige est épaisse et charge un sol glacé!

Quand seul dans un ciel pâle un peuplier s'élance,
Quand sous le manteau blanc qui vient de le cacher
L'immobile corbeau sur l'arbre se balance,
Comme la girouette au bout du long clocher!

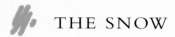 # THE SNOW

How lovely are the stories
  That tell of long ago
When all the trees are barren
  And heavy lies the snow
  On iron earth below!

When on the pallid skyline
  The lonely poplar-tree
Leaps up, and there the raven
  Snow-pied sits solemnly
  As though a vane were he!

How lovely are the stories
  That tell of long ago
When all the trees are leafless
  And earth lies frore below
  Her coverlid of snow!

Alfred de Vigny, 'La Neige' from Poèmes
antiques et modernes *(1826),*
tr. W. Thorley

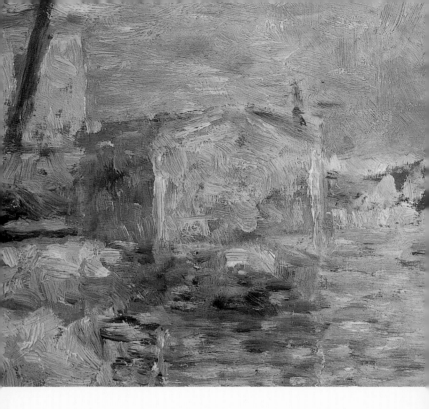

 DUSK

Morn is no more, nor yet the twilight trembles,
    Though from our eyes love's paling splendours flee.

But rosy dusk the rosy dawn resembles,
    And, with Night's shadow, shall oblivion be!

Gérard de Nerval, 'Ni bonjour ni bonsoir', from Petits
châteaux de Bohème *(1853), tr. W. J. Robertson*

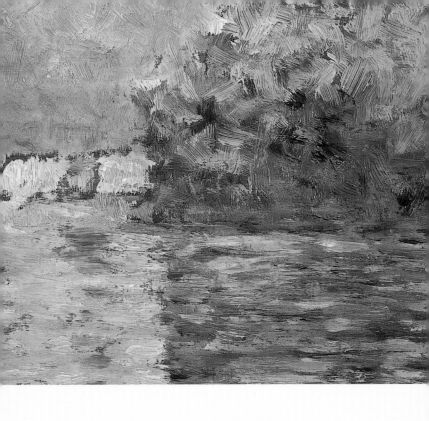

Le matin n'est plus! le soir pas encore:
Pourtant de nos yeux l'éclair a pâli.

Mais le soir vermeil ressemble à l'aurore,
Et la nuit plus tard amène l'oubli!

AFTER THREE YEARS

I pushed the gate that swung so silently,
   And I was in the garden and aware
   Of early daylight on the flowers there
And cups of dew sun-kindled. I could see
Nothing was changed from what it used to be.
   There was the wild-vine arbour, the old chair
   The fountain singing silverly in air,
The eternal sigh of the old aspen-tree.

And still the rose is fluttering; as before
   The tall, proud lily sways in the warm breeze;
I know the very larks that sink or soar;
   And even the statue, frail amid her trees,
With plaster crumbling on the grassy floor,
   Shines amid shadows of dead fragrancies.

Paul Verlaine, 'Après Trois Ans',
from Poèmes saturniens
(1866), tr. W. Thorley

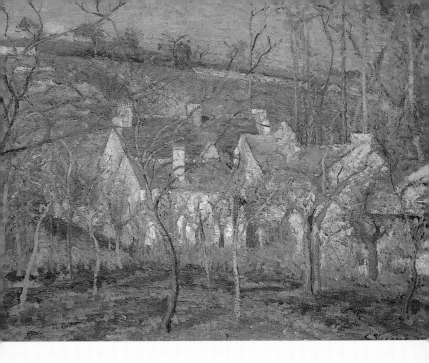

Ayant poussé la porte étroite qui chancelle
Je me suis promené dans le petit jardin
Qu'éclairait doucement le soleil du matin,
Pailletant chaque fleur d'une humide étincelle.

Rien n'a changé. J'ai tout revu: l'humble tonnelle
De vigne folle avec les chaises de rotin . . .
Le jet d'eau fait toujours son murmure argentin
Et le vieux tremble sa plainte sempiternelle.

Les roses comme avant palpitent; comme avant,
Les grands lys orgueilleux se balancent au vent.
Chaque alouette qui va et vient m'est connue.

Même j'ai retrouvé debout la Velléda
Dont le plâtre s'écaille au bout de l'avenue,
– Grêle, parmi l'odeur fade du réséda.

25

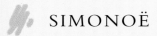

SIMONOË

Simonoë, the snow is white as the pure white skin
Of thy two knees or the whiteness under your chin.

Simonoë, thy hand is cold as the white snow is;
Simonoë, thy heart likewise is as cold as this.

Only a kiss of fire turns the snow to rain,
And only a farewell kiss makes thy heart fain.

The snow is sad on boughs that the tall pines bear;
Thy brow is sad in the shadow of thy gold hair.

Flight-weary, thy sister the snow sleeps there like a dove;
Simonoë, thou art my snow and my heart's dear love.

Remy de Gourmont, 'La Neige', from
Simone (1901), tr. W. Thorley.

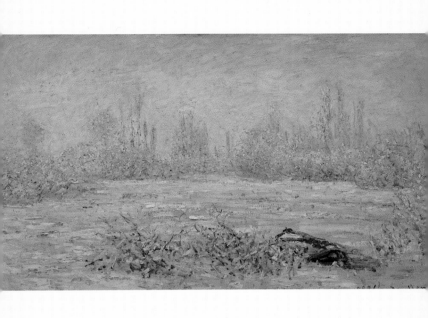

Simone, la neige est blanche comme ton cou.
Simone, la neige est blanche comme tes genoux.

Simone, ta main est froide comme la neige,
Simone, ton cœur est froid comme la neige,

La neige ne fond qu'a un baiser de feu,
Ton cœur ne fond qu'a un baiser d'adieu.

La neige est triste sœur les branches de pin,
Ton front est triste sous tes cheveux chatains.

Simone, ta sœur la neige dort dans la cour,
Simone, tu es ma neige et mon amour.

THE VALLEY

My heart, in which even hope has ceased to live,
Shall weary fate no more with idle breath;
Give me, O valley of my childhood, give
Me shelter for a day to wait on death!

Here the straight pathway leaves the open glade:
Along its devious slopes hang the dense boughs
That, bending over me their mingled shade,
With blissful calm and silence crown my brows.

Alphonse de Lamartine, 'Le Vallon', from Méditations
poétiques *(1820), tr. W. J. Robertson*

Mon cœur, lassé de tout, même de l'espérance,
N'ira plus de ses vœux importuner le sort;
Prêtez-moi seulement, vallons de mon enfance,
Un asile d'un jour pour attendre la mort.

Voici l'étroit sentier de l'obscure vallée:
Du flanc de ces coteaux pendent des bois épais
Qui, courbant sur mon front leur ombre entremêlée,
Me couvrent tout entier de silence et de paix.

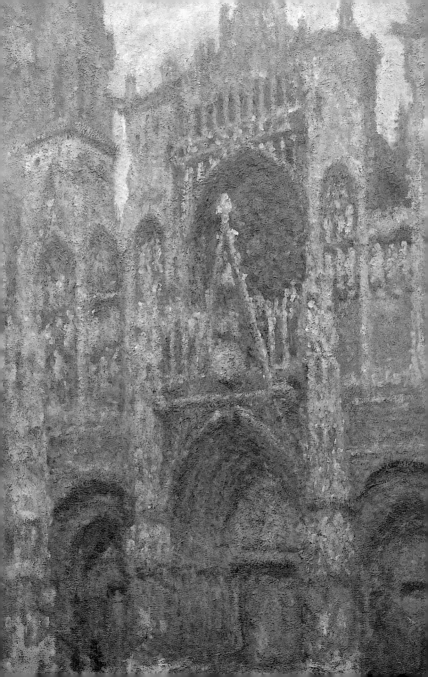

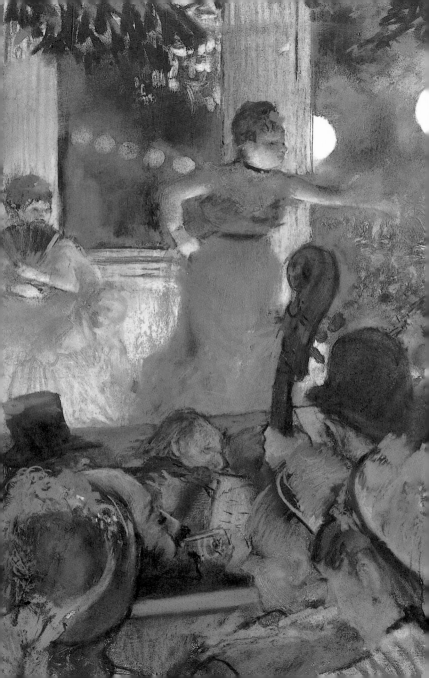

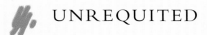

UNREQUITED

Thine air, thy head, thy gesture,
Nothing to call thee after
But, in thine own investure
A being made of laughter.

The colour to thy pale cheek rushing
Dazzles all beholders.
This passes into blushing
Of naked arms and shoulders.

That shifting colour, know it's
A serpent's in the valley,
That in the mind of Poets
Evokes a flowerless Ballet.

These mad clothes, they are jolly,
Thy spirit seems to await thee;
Thou fool to mine own folly,
I love thee as I hate thee.

Charles Baudelaire, 'A celle qui est trop gai',
from Les Fleurs du Mal *(1857),*
tr. A. Symons

Ta tête, ton geste, ton air
Sont beaux comme un beau paysage;
Le rire joue en ton visage
Comme un vent frais dans un ciel clair.

Le passant chagrin que tu frôles
Est ébloui par la santé
Qui jaillit comme une clarté
De tes bras et de tes épaules.

Les retentissantes couleurs
Dont tu parsèmes tes toilettes
Jettent dans l'esprit des poètes
L'image d'un ballet de fleurs.

Ces robes folles sont l'emblème
De ton esprit bariolé;
Folle dont je suis affolé,
Je te hais autant que je t'aime!

TWO WAYS

Two ways hath Life. One as a stream
With flowers environed quits the source,
The even tenor of its course
Scarce ruffled by the transient gleam
No echo marks the onward roll
Of waters without plaint or sigh,
That win scant heed from passers-by,
But still unhastening reach the goal.

One as a torrent unconfined
Breaks headlong forth with frenzied will;
No agency its rage can still,
No barriers curb, no forces bind.
The first achieves, the second aims;
One limits hath, the other none,
Each day its task afresh begun –
Patience, Ambition, are their names.

Alfred de Musset, from La Coupe et les lèvres
(1832), tr. M. Betham-Edwards.

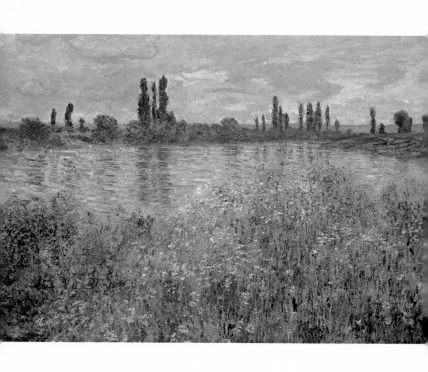

Il est deux routes dans la vie:
L'une solitaire et fleurie,
Qui descend sa pente chérie
Sans se plaindre et sans soupirer.
Le passant la remarque à peine,
Comme le ruisseau de la plaine,
Que le sable de la fontaine
Ne fait pas même murmurer.
L'autre, comme un torrent sans digue,
Dans une éternelle fatigue,
Sous les pieds de l'enfant prodigue
Roule la pierre d'Ixion.
L'une est bornée et l'autre immense;
L'une meurt où l'autre commence;
La première est la patience,
La seconde est l'ambition.

NOON

Noon, with all summer for kingdom, throws over the plain
Swathings of silver that now from the zenith down beat.
Now is the air all dumbfounded with fiery rain;
Earth in her flame-woven vesture is drowsy with heat.

For, far away are the fields with no shadowy blur;
Dry is the spring that once ran, a cool boon for the kine;
For, far away looms the dark of the woods without stir
Where in a leaden deep slumber the branches recline.

Charles-Marie-René Leconte de Lisle, 'Midi', from
Poésies complètes (1858), tr. W. Thorley

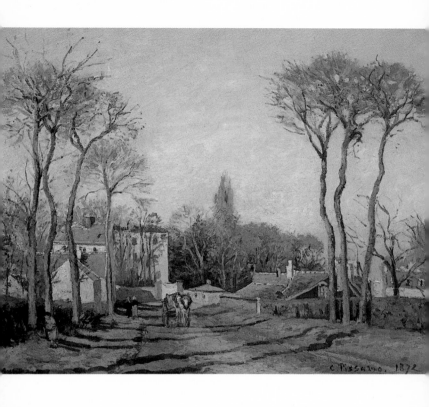

Midi, Roi des étés, épandu sur la plaine,
Tombe en nappes d'argent des hauteurs du ciel bleu.
Tout se tait. L'air flamboie et brûle sans haleine;
La Terre est assoupie en sa robe de feu.

L'étendue est immense, et les champs n'ont point d'ombre,
Et la source est tarie où buvaient les troupeaux;
La lointaine forêt, dont la lisière est sombre,
Dort là-bas, immobile, en un pesant repos.

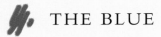

THE BLUE

The eternal Blue, remote, serene, unkind,
O'erwhelms with beauty as of idle flowers
The poet groping with his weight of mind
Through arid wastes of unassuagèd hours.

Waif, with shut eyes I feel the piercing look
Of its keen sys strike down my soul's void space.
Where shall I fly? How foil the sharp rebuke
In darkness unbeholden of its face?

Rise, mists! Pour out your slow, sad, ashen breath!
With rags of haze festoon the skiey roof
To o'erbrim the marsh where autumn loitereth
And tear a throne of silence far aloof.

And then, dear Grief, from pools of Lethe's tide
Steal out and pluck the ooze-filled rushe's blade
With hand unwearied weave a veil to hide
The huge blue rents the heartless birds have made.

Stéphane Mallarmé, 'L'Azur',
from Poésies *(1899), tr. W. Thorley*

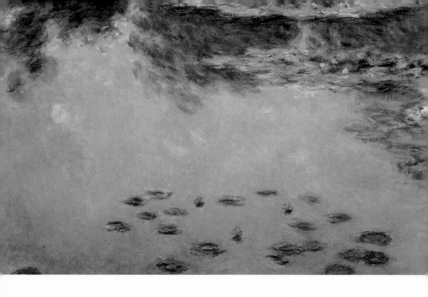

De l'éternel Azur la sereine ironie
Accable, belle indolemment comme les fleurs,
Le poète impuissant qui maudit son génie
À travers un désert stérile de Douleurs.

Fuyant, les yeux fermés, je le sens qui regarde,
Avec l'intensité d'un remords atterrant,
Mon âme vide. Où fuir? Et quelle nuit hagarde
Jeter, lambeaux, jeter sur ce mépris navrant?

Brouillards, montez! Versez vos cendres monotones
Avec de longs haillons de brume dans les cieux
Qui noiera le marais livide des automnes,
Et bâtissez un grand plafond silencieux!

Et toi, sors des étangs léthéens et ramasse
En t'en venant la vase et les pâles roseaux,
Cher Ennui, pour boucher d'une main jamais lasse
Les grands trous bleus que font méchamment les oiseaux.

L'étendue est immense, et les champs n'ont point d'ombre,
Et la source est tarie où buvaient les troupeaux;
La lointaine forêt, dont la lisière est sombre,
Dort là-bas, immobile, en un pesant repos.

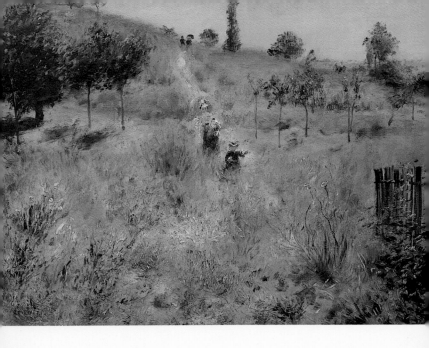

Voici venir les temps où vibrant sur sa tige
Chaque fleur s'évapore ainsi qu'un encensoir;
Les sons et les parfums tournent dans l'air du soir;
Valse mélancolique et langoureux vertige!

Chaque fleur s'évapore ainsi qu'un encensoir;
Le violon frémit comme un cœur qu'on afflige;
Valse mélancolique et langoureux vertige!
Le ciel est triste et beau comme un grand reposoir.

Le violon frémit comme un cœur qu'on afflige,
Un cœur tendre, qui hait le néant vaste et noir!
Le ciel est triste et beau comme un grand reposoir;
Le soleil s'est noyé dans son sang qui se fige.

Un cœur tendre, qui hait le néant vaste et noir,
Du passé lumineux recueille tout vestige!
Le soleil s'est noyé dans son sang qui se fige . . .
Ton souvenir en moi luit comme un ostensoir!

HARMONIES OF THE EVENING

Now is the hour when, trembling to and fro,
All flowers like censers waft their odours sweet,
And scents in evening air, and music meet
A solemn waltz, a languorous vertigo.

All flowers like censers waft their odours sweet,
The viol shudders as a heart in woe,
A solemn waltz, a languorous veritgo,
The heavens stretch fair and sad like some great sheet.

The viol shudders as a heart in woe,
Kind heart that hates black nothingness to meet,
The heavens stretch fair and sad like some great sheet.
The sun sinks, drowning, in his sanguine glow.

Kind heart that hates black nothingness to meet,
On the bright past doth pensive love bestow;
The sun sinks, drowning, in his sanguine glow;
Thy memory, hallowed shrine, my soul does greet.

Charles Baudelaire, 'Harmonie du soir',
from Les Fleurs du Mal *(1857),*
tr. H. Carrington

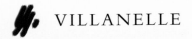 VILLANELLE

When warmth and sunshine come again,
And cold and gloom are gone for good,
Then, Love! to pick the flowers we twain
Will go together in the wood,
Brushing the pearls beneath our feet,
Formed by the sun and early dew,
And listen to the thrushes sweet,
    Their song renew.

Now, Love! we welcome back the Spring:
This month is the true lover's tide;
The bird now preens his satin wing,
And sings of love his nest beside.
Come, then, to the moss bank away,
And how we love tell o'er and o'er,
And let me hear you softly say
    For evermore.

A long, long ramble let us take,
The hidden rabbit cause to fly.
And watch the stag within the lake
Gaze on his antlers wide and high.
Then, after long delightful hours,
Homeward with fingers intertwined,
Bear strawberries and forest flowers
    Together found.

Théophile Gautier, 'Villanelle rythmique',
from La Comédie de la Mort
(1838), tr. H. Carrington

Quand viendra la saison nouvelle,
Quand auront disparu les froids,
Tous les deux nous irons, ma belle,
Pour cueillir le muguet aux bois;
Sous nos pieda égrenant les perles
Que l'on voit au matin trembler
Nous irons écouter les merles
   Siffler.

Le printemps est venu, ma belle,
C'est le mois des amants béni,
Et l'oiseau, satinant son aile,
Dit ses vers au rebord du nid.
Oh! viens donc, sur ce banc de mousse
Pour parler de nos beaux amours,
Et dis-moi de ta voix si douce:
   'Toujours!'

Loin, bien loin, égarant nos courses,
Faisant fuir le lapin caché
Et le daim au miroir des sources
Admirant son grand bois penché,
Puis, chez nous, tout heureux, tout aises,
En panier enlaçant nos doigts,
Revenons rapportant des fraises
   Des bois.

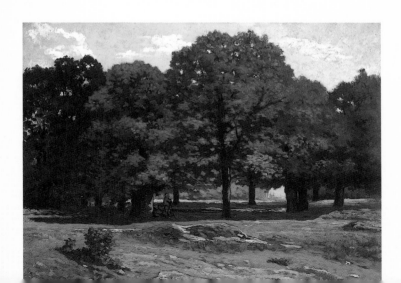

LANDSCAPE

From poplars shuddering in their leafy swoon
As though therefrom a flock of birds took flight
There falls each separate image, sole and slight,
On the dim mirror of the drowsed lagoon.
Flush with the dark wall, lo! the full round moon
Swerves from the bridge, and with her silver light
Clear and aloof, in sadness infinite
Mounts thro' the sky to her unclouded noon.

By fields and lane the hedgerow falls the spell
Of gloaming nights that only dream can give;
No laggard hell along the causey rings.
Yet doth the fickle air grow voluble,
While sole and constant thro' the flooded sieve
The loud weir-water to the twilight sings.

Henri de Régnier, tr. W. Thorley

De hauts peupliers dont le feuillage frémit
Comme si des oiseaux y prenaient leurs volées
Reflétent, un à un, leurs tiges isolées
Dans le fuyant miroir du canal endormi;

Au-dessus du vieux pont courbant son arche unique,
Au ras du parapet noir, la lune, émergeant
Dans sa rondeur et dans son éclat mat d'argent
Monte dans le ciel clair, calme et mélancolique.

Alentour, sur les champs, les routes, les buisssons,
S'épandent des lueurs douces de nuits rêvées;
Nul pas humaine ne va sonant sur les levées.

Et pourtant, l'air est plein d'impalpables frissons,
Et, là-bas, très distinct en ces rumeurs confuses,
Chante l'écoulement de l'eau dans les écluses.

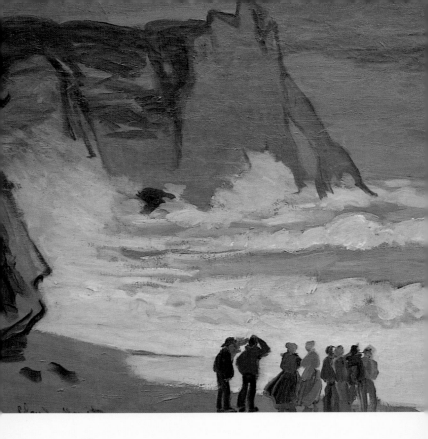

 BITTERNESS

You are an autumnal sky the spirit knows!
Sadness within me rises like the sea,
And leaves, in its ebbing, on my lip morose
The bitterness of inexorable misery.

Charles Baudelaire, 'Causerie',
from Les Fleurs du Mal
(1857), tr. A. Symons

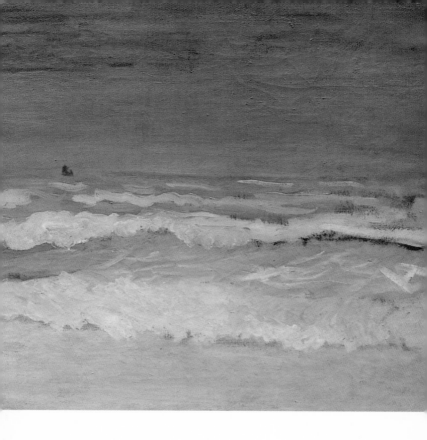

Vous êtes un beau ciel d'automne, clair et rose!
Mais la tristesse en moi monte comme la mer,
Et laisse, en refluant, sur ma lèvre morose
Le souvenir cuisant de son limon amer.

45

THE BOURGEOIS

The world since it exists we tolerate,
Let us consider men devoid of hate –
That Bourgeois, product of our age behold:
Eggs, cheese, and soap in former days he sold;
Now he is rich, has vineyard, field, and wood;
The poor he hates, and loves not noble blood;
A porter's son, he deems it vain to trace
From Montmorency's ancient dukes your race.
He is austere, and virtuous, and discreet;
Having, when cold, warm carpets 'neath his feet,
He holds with order than can wealth protect;
Lovers he hates, and men of intellect.
He gives some alms, he lends on usury;
And says – of progress and pure liberty,
Of rights of nations – 'Sweep such rubbish hence!'
He has good Sancho's coarse, rough common sense.
He let Cervantes die for want of aid;
He praises Boileau. He'll caress a maid
And while with him intriguing, loudly cries
'Gainst novels for their immoralities.

Victor Hugo, 'Le Soutien des empires', from Les Quatres
Vents de l'esprit *(1881), tr. H. Carrington*

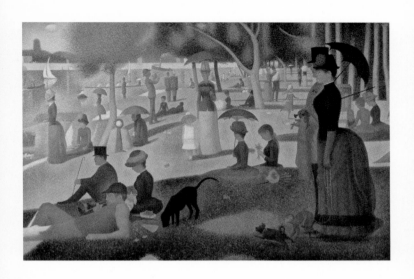

Puisque ce monde existe, il sied qu'on le tolère.
Sachons considérer les êtres sans colère.
Cet homme est le bourgeois du siècle où nous vivons.
Autrefois il vendait des suifs et des savons,
Maintenant il est riche; il a prés, bois, vignobles.
Il déteste le peuple, il n'aime pas les nobles;
Étant fils d'un portier, il trouve en ce temps-ci
Inutile qu'on soit fils des Montmorency.
Il est sévère. Il est vertueux. Il est membre,
Ayant de bons tapis sous les pieds en décembre,
Du grand parti de l'ordre et des honnêtes gens.
Il hait les amoureux et les intelligents;
Il fait un peu l'aumône, il fait un peu l'usure;
Il dit du progrès saint, de la liberté pure,
Du droit des nations: je ne veux pas de ça!
Il a ce gros bon sens du cher Sancho Pança
Qui laisserait mourir à l'hôpital Cervantes;
Il admire Boileau, caresse les servantes,
Et crie, après avoir chiffonné Jeanneton,
À l'immoralité du roman feuilleton.

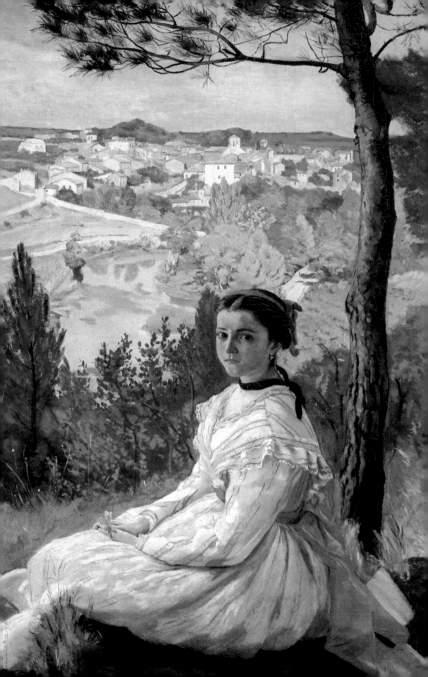

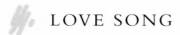 LOVE SONG

Who will, before the break of day,
To him my soul adores repair;
Because for love I pine away,
The secret of my flame to bear.

O Heart! to what safe heart and true
Canst trust thy message to be borne?
For if the lark my secret knew,
She'd go and tell it to the morn

Théodore de Banville, 'Chanson d'amour',
from Les Stalactites *(1844), tr. H. Carrington*

Qui veut avant le point du jour,
Vers le bien-aimé de mon âme,
Parce que je languis d'amour,
Porter le secret de ma flamme?

O mon cœur, à quel cœur discret
Peux-tu te confier encore? –
Si l'alouette a mon secret,
Elle ira le dire à l'Aurore.

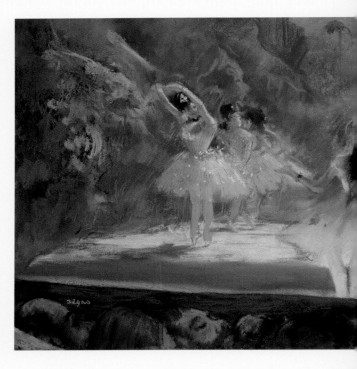

 GRANDFATHER'S SONG

Dance, little girls,
All in a ring;
To see you so pretty,
The forest will sing.

Dance, little Queens,
All in a ring;
Loves to Lasses
Sweet kisses will bring.

Victor Hugo, 'Chanson de grand-père', from L'art
d'être grand-père *(1877), tr. H. Carrington*

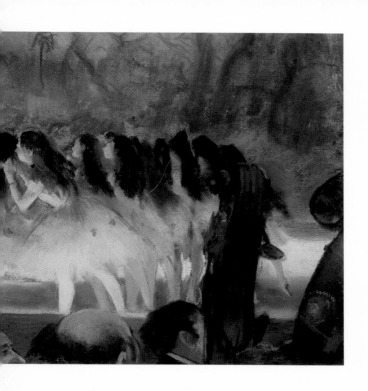

Dansez, les petites filles,
Toutes en rond.
En vous voyant si gentilles,
Les bois riront.

Dansez, les petites reines,
Toutes en rond.
Les amoureux sous les frênes
S'embrasseront.

WHAT IS POETRY?

Building verses to eternize
Momentary phantasies,
Wooing beauty, goodness, truth,
Never parting with his youth,
But haphazard, grave or gay,
Laughing, weeping, on his way;
Little nothings as he goes
All sufficing for his muse,
Into pearls transmuting tears,
Thus the poet spends his years.
Such the passion and the dream
That the poet best beseem!

Alfred de Musset, 'Impromptu',
tr. M. Betham-Edwards

Chasser tout souvenir et fixer sa pensée,
Sur un bel axe d'or la tenir balancée,
Incertaine, inquiète, immobile pourtant,
Peut-être éterniser le rêve d'un instant;

Aimer le vrai, le beau, chercher leur harmonie;
Écouter dans son cœur l'écho de son génie;
Chanter, rire, pleurer, seul, sans but, au hasard;
D'un sourire, d'un mot, d'un soupir, d'un regard

Faire un travail exquis, plein de crainte et de charme
Faire une perle d'une larme:
Du poète ici-bas voilà la passion,
Voilà son bien, sa vie et son ambition.

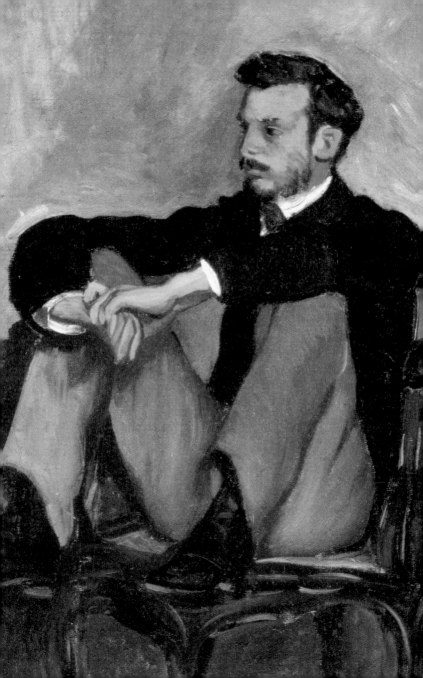

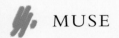 MUSE

Poor soul, what word comes from thy loneliness,
What word, my heart, remembering old mischance,
Unto that utter Beauty that can bless
Anew thy being with her godlike glance?
'Her do we praise with our proud melodies
There is naught sweeter than her sacred might
Whose flesh is scented as an angel's is,
Whose glance clothes all things in unstainèd light.

Whether it be in darkness where non bide
Or in the sunlit street by many trod,
Her ghost goes fluttering like a flame in air.
She saith: "I, who am lovely, bid thee guide
Thy heart to follow Beauty everywhere,
I who am Angel, Muse and Mother of God!"'

Charles Baudelaire, 'Que diras-tu ce soir, pauvre âme solitaire'
from Les Fleurs du Mal *(1857), tr. W. Thorley*

Que diras-tu ce soir, pauvre âme solitaire,
Que diras-tu, mon cœur, cœur autrefois flétri,
À la très belle, à la très bonne, à la très chère,
Dont le regard divin t'a soudain refleuri?
— Nous mettrons notre orgueil à chanter ses louanges:
Rien ne vaut la douceur de son autorité
Sa chair spirituelle a le parfum des Anges
Et son œil nous revêt d'un habit de clarté.
Que ce soit dans la nuit et dans la solitude
Que ce soit dans la rue et dans la multitude
Son fantôme dans l'air danse comme un flambeau.
Parfois il parle et dit: 'Je suis belle, et j'ordonne
Que pour l'amour de moi vous n'aimiez que le Beau;
Je suis l'Ange gardien, la Muse et la Madone.'

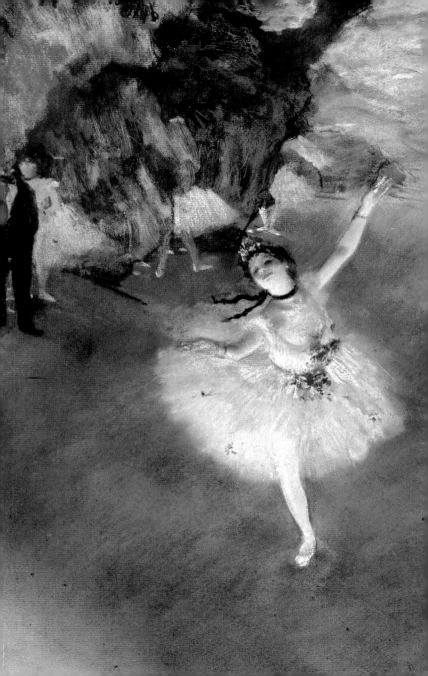

Comme le matin rit sur les roses en pleurs!
Oh! les charmants petits amoureux qu'ont les fleurs!
Ce n'est dans les jasmins, ce n'est dans les pervenches
Qu'un éblouissement de folles ailes blanches
Qui vont, viennent, s'en vont, reviennent, se fermant,
Se rouvrant, dans un vaste et doux frémissement.
O printemps! quand on songe à toutes les missives
Qui des amants rêveurs vont aux belles pensives,
A ces cœurs confiés au papier, à ce tas
De lettres que le feutre écrit au taffetas,
Au message d'amour, d'ivresse et de délire
Qu'on reçoit en avril et qu'en met l'on déchire,
On croit voir s'envoler, au gré du vent joyeux,
Dans les prés, dans les bois, sur les eaux, dans les cieux,
Et rôder en tous lieux, cherchant partout une âme,
Et courir à la fleur en sortant de la femme,
Les petits morceaux blancs, chassés en tourbillons
De tous les billets doux, devenus papillons.

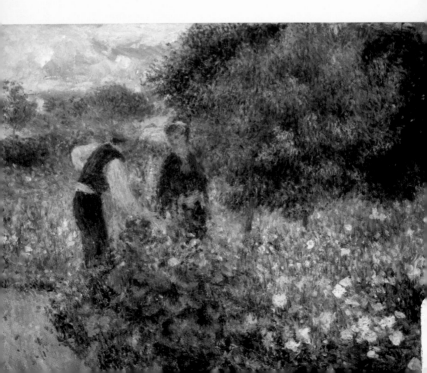

BUTTERFLIES

Now the weeping roses the dawn's welcome take!
What darling lovers the sweet flowers make!
Now are jasmine and the periwinkle
With endless tumult of white wings a-twinkle
That come and go, now wafted, now alit
With wings close-folded ere again they flit
In one vast impulse. Spring-time! Do but ponder
On wistful lovers who, when they were fonder,
Poured out their hearts on paper! How they thrilled
With eager vows, their panting bosoms spilled
In messages of April – town and flouted
Ere on their stems the shy June rosebuds pouted!
Thus you behold in all those white wings there
By wood and lawn, and up in the glad air –
Seeking from flow'r to flow'r with love's sweet aching
A mate more dear than her they are foresaking –
The litter of sweet love-notes that arise
In ardent eddies of white butterflies.

Victor Hugo, 'Vere Novo', from
Les Contemplations
(1856), tr. W. Thorley

EPITAPH

Comrades, whensoe'er I die;
A willow set my grave to keep;
I love its soft pale livery
And drooping boughs that seem to weep;
And lightly will its shadow lie
On the ground where I shall sleep.

Alfred de Musset, 'Elegie', tr. H. Carrington

Mes chers amis, quand je mourrai
Plantez un saule au cimetière.
J'aime son feuillage éploré;
La pâleur m'en est douce et chère,
Et son ombre sera légère
À la terre où je dormirai.

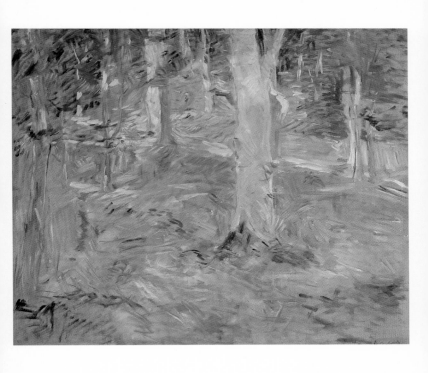

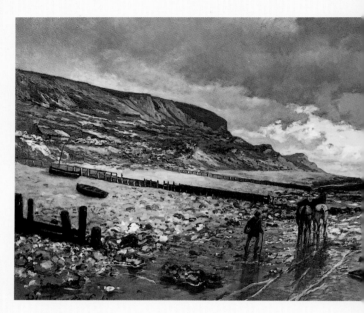

 AUTUMN

The long-drawn sighs
Like violin-cries,
   Of autumn wailing,
Lull in my soul
The languorous shoal
   Of thoughts assailing.

Wan, as whom knells
Of funeral bells
   Bemoan and banish,
I weep upon
Days dead and gone
   With dreams that vanish;

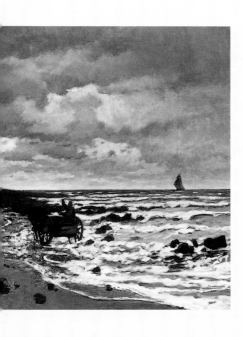

Les sanglots longs
Des violons
De l'automne
Blessent mon cœur
D'une langueur
Monotone.

Tout suffocant
Et blême, quand
Sonne l'heure,
Je me souviens
Des jours anciens
Et je pleure;

Et je m'en vais
Au vent mauvais
Qui m'emporte
Deça, delà
Pareil à la
Feuille morte.

The helpless swing
On the wind's wing;
  Tossed hither and thither
As winter sweeps
From swirling heaps
  Worn leaves that wither.

Paul Verlaine, 'Chanson d'automne',
from Poèmes saturniens *(1866),*
tr. W. J. Robertson

INVOCATION

To her the dearest, loveliest,
Who light into my bosom sends,
Idol and angel, ever blest,
Be health and life that never ends.

Into my life herself she pours,
As air impregnate of the sea,
An to my craving soul restores
The longings for Eternity.

Perfume that ever fresh doth spread
Its fragrance through some dear retreat;
Forgotten censer that doth shed
Through night a secret incense sweet.

O Love, whose nature death defies,
How can I picture what thou art?
Sweet grain of musk that hidden lies
Deathless and deep within my heart.

To her most beautiful and best,
Who does my bliss and life supply,
Idol and angel, ever blest,
Be health and immortality.

Charles Baudelaire, 'Hymne', from Les Fleurs
du Mal *(1857), tr. H. Carrington*

A la très chère, à la très belle
Qui remplit mon cœur de clarté,
A l'ange, à l'idole immortelle,
Salut en immortalité!

Elle se répand dans ma vie
Comme un air imprégné de sel,
Et dans mon âme inassouvie,
Verse le goût de l'éternel.

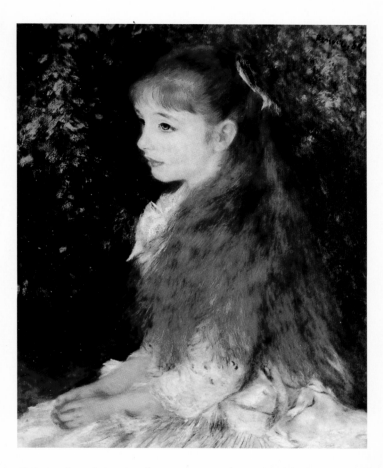

Sachet toujours frais qui parfume
L'atmosphère d'un cher réduit,
Encensoir oublié qui fume
En secret à travers la nuit,

Comment, amour incorruptible,
T'exprimer avec vérité?
Grain de musc qui gis, invisible,
Au fond de mon éternité!

A l'ange, à l'idole immortelle,
A la très bonne, à la très belle
Qui fait ma joie et ma santé,
Salut en immortalité!

63

ON THE SIERRA

I love the glorious mountains, proud and bleak!
No tree, not e'en a flower, does set its foot
On the white shroud that clothes the lofty peak,
Whose bare crags give no holding to a root.

No vine's love-clinging arm, no golden wheat,
Nothing that tells of man and servile toil;
In the pure air and free, sail eagles fleet,
no vulgar sound their majesty to spoil.

They are not useful. True! No profit yield
Their might, their beauty is their only boast;
Yet please me more than the fat fertile field
So far from heaven, that sight of God is lost.

Théophile Gautier, 'Dans la sierra', from
España *(1845), tr. H. Carrington*

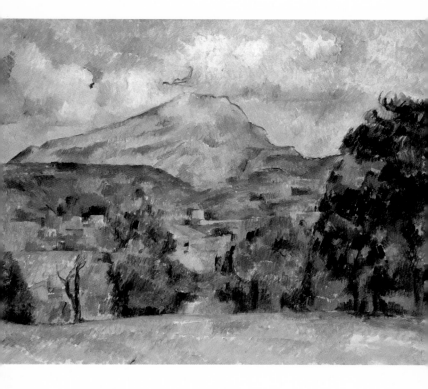

J'aime d'un fol amour les monts fiers et sublimes!
Les plantes n'osent pas poser leurs pieds frileux
Sur le linceul d'argent qui recouvre leurs cimes;
Le soc s'émousserait à leurs pics anguleux.

Ni vigne aux bras lascifs, ni blés dorés, ni seigles;
Rien qui rappelle l'homme et le travail maudit.
Dans leur air libre et pur nagent des essaims d'aigles,
Et l'écho du rocher siffle l'air du bandit.

Ils ne rapportent rien et ne sont pas utiles;
Ils n'ont que leur beauté, je le sais, c'est bien peu;
Mais, moi, je les préfère aux champs gras et fertiles,
Qui sont si loin du ciel qu'on n'y voit jamais Dieu!

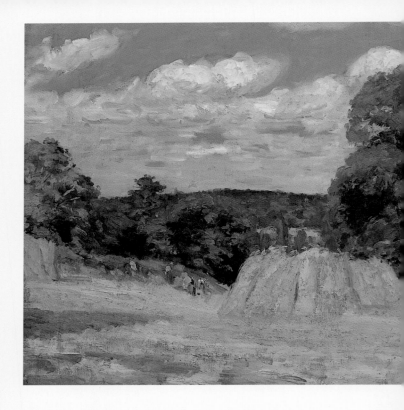

 HYMN TO THE EARTH

Her throne is the meadow, the field and the plain,
She is dear to the sowers and reapers of grain,
    To the shepherds that sleep on the heather;
She warms her chill breast in the fires of the suns
And laughs, when with stars in their circle she runs,
    As with sisters rejoicing together.

Victor Hugo, 'La Terre: Une Hymne', from
La Légende des siècles *(1877), tr. W. J. Robertson*

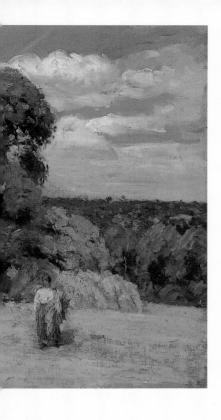

Elle est la terre, elle est la plaine, elle est le champ.
Elle est chère à tous ceux qui sèment en marchant;
Elle offre un lit de mousse au pâtre;
Frileuse, elle se chauffe au soleil éternel,
Rit, et fait cercle avec les planètes du ciel
Comme des sœurs autour de l'âtre.

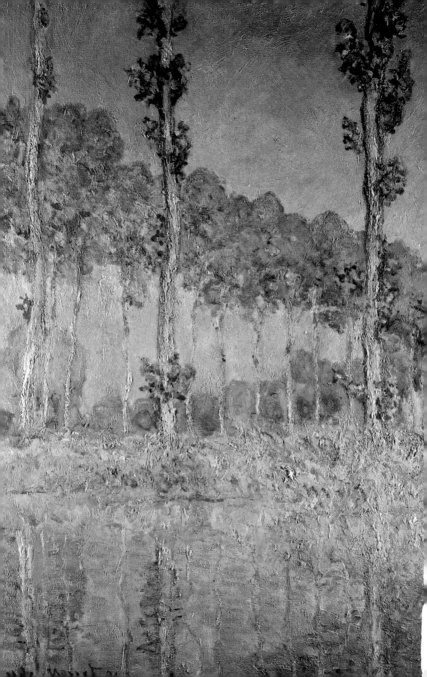

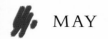 MAY

'Twas on a bright, warm afternoon in May
I chanced beside a pleasant stream to stray,
Where every fleeting cloud was mirrored back.
I followed slowly whither led the track
Profuse with flowers, and sloping towards the edge
Slim reeds and poplars either margin hedge.

> François Coppée, 'Le vieux soulier',
> from Le Cahier rouge (1874),
> tr. H. Carrington

> En mai, par une pure et chaude après-midi,
> Je cheminais au bord d'un doux fleuve attiédi
> Où se réfléchissait la fuite d'un nuage.
> Je suivais lentement le chemin de halage
> Tout en fleurs, qui descend en pente vers les eaux.
> Des peupliers à droite, à gauche des roseaux.

ABOUT THE POETS

Théodore de Banville (1823–91) wrote four books of
poetry, including his masterpiece *Odes funamblesques* (1857),
which was dedicated to Victor Hugo. He devoted the later part
of his life mainly to criticism.

Charles Baudelaire (1821–67) was the greatest French poet
of the nineteenth-century. His revolutionary modern style, his
frank and uncompromising exploration of the human heart
and his mastery of imagery were hugely influential. His
principal work, *Les Fleurs du mal* caused such a scandal that
legal proceedings led to six of the poems being excised from
the collection. In addition to producing poetry and other
literary works, he was a prolific art critic, championing
Delacroix, Courbet and the realists, and later the impressionists.

François Coppée (1842–1908) was a leading Parnassian poet
and playwright. Parnassians preferred a more austere, classical
and polished style of poetry to the emotionally charged
excesses of Romanticism. Because of his preoccuaption with
the emotions of ordinary folk, Coppée became known as the
poète des humbles.

Théophile Gautier (1811–72) started out as a painter before
turning to poetry, writing high Romantic works such as the
Comédie de la mort (The Comedy of Death). His tenet of 'art
for art's sake' became a chief inspiration for writers of the
Parnassian school.

While holding the post of Deputy Minister of Finance
Armand Gouffé (1775–1845) was a singer and writer
of poems, songs and vaudeville sketches. His joyful works
celebrate wine and fine food, although ill-health precluded
him from indulging those appetites himself.

Remy de Gourmont (1858–1915) wrote literary criticism for *Le Monde* and other periodicals. In the later part of his life, he developed a skin disease and lived as a recluse, producing Symbolist poems and novels of great complexity, as well as scholarly essays.

Victor Hugo (1802–85) is best known for his epic novels *Les Misérables* and *Nôtre Dame de Paris*, but was not only a prolific and versatile dramatist and poet at the forefront of the Romantic movement but also a leading statesman and politician. Acclaimed as a national hero in his own lifetime, he was buried in the Panthéon.

Alphonse de Lamartine (1790–1869) turned to poetry during lulls in his military and political careers, with his work frequently inspired by foreign places. His *Meditations* on faith and despair are in perfect keeping with the Romantic project, though the poems stick to conventionally classical forms.

Charles-Marie-René Leconte de Lisle (1818–94) was born on the island of Reunion. His poems, full of gravity, classicism and local exotic colour, are known best for their deeply pessimistic tone.

Stéphane Mallarmé (1842–98) was a leader of the Symbolist school of French poetry, which sought to express states of the soul purely through imagery. His best-known poem *L'Après-midi d'un faune* inspired the orchestral work of the same name by Claude Debussy.

Alfred de Musset (1810–57) was a prolific author of poems, plays and novels. His best work is poised between Classical and Romantic impulses. In his autobiographical novel *Confession d'un enfant du siècle* (1836) he gives an account of his affair with George Sand.

The eccentric **Gérard de Nerval** (1808–55) is often seen as a precursor to Symbolist and Surrealist writers. He wrote poems, plays, essays and short stories, and translated and expanded Goethe's *Faust* into French.

Henri de Régnier (1884–1936) began as a Parnassian, but later soon converted to Symbolism. He was one of the pioneers of what is today known as 'free verse'.

Paul Verlaine (1844–96) was associated initially with the Parnassian poets. However, over the course of his tumultuous relationship with Arthur Rimbaud, he experimented with irregular forms. Many contemporary composers were inspired to set his poems to music.

The expression 'shut up in an ivory tower' was first coined by the critic Saint-Beuve in 1837 to describe **Alfred de Vigny** (1797–1863), whose pessimistic philosophy led him to advocate a detachment of art from society.

THE IMPRESSIONIST GARDEN

It is hard for us today to imagine the shock and outrage that was generated by the first exhibition of impressionist art in Paris in April 1874. The paintings, by fifty-five artists including Cézanne, Degas, Manet, Monet, Pissarro and Renoir, were radical, consciously breaking every rule of artistic propriety. Their subject matter consisted of trivial, workaday scenes; their compositions appeared lop-sided or truncated; they looked unfinished, with no attempt made to hide the rapidly-executed brushwork. Most alarmingly, they made use of a radically new palette of pure colours in bold juxtapositions. The radiant dance of hues that modern viewers find so beguiling, to nineteenth-century eyes was eccentric and unharmonious.

Such wholesale disregard for tradition amounted to artistic anarchy, and the public greeted their works with either bemusement or open hostility. The critic Louis Leroy popularized the derogatory term 'impressionist', referring to Monet's painting *Sunrise: An Impression*, though the artists themselves preferred to refer to themselves simply as 'independents'.

Although the impressionists had a wide range of preoccupations and personalities, the two principal themes that united the their paintings and gave them their immediacy were their modern subject matter and their interest in the fleeting effects of light.

An early champion of the impressionists, the poet Charles Baudelaire wrote in *The Painter of Modern Life* (1863):

Modernity is the transient, the fleeting, the contingent; it is one half of art, the other being the eternal and the immovable. There was a form of modernity for every painter of the past; the majority of the fine portraits that remain to us from former times are clothed in the dress of their own day. They are perfectly harmonious works because the dress, the hairstyle, and even the gesture, the expression and the smile (each age has its carriage, its expression and its smile) form a whole, full of vitality.

The impressionists' aim of raising transient glimpses of modern life to the status of high art was perfectly in accord with Baudelaire's injunction. Seeking to escape the stultifying atmosphere of the studio and academy, they worked direct from life, in the open air or in cafés, workplaces, even railway stations. The impressionists were the visual poets of modern Parisian life.

However, it was perhaps in order to develop further their new theories of colour that many impressionists sought contemporary subject matter away from the mud and smoke of the city. Their vision of the countryside was not the wild nature as Romantic artists had portrayed it, but suburban landscapes, farms, seaside resorts and gardens. This was nature tamed by man, used for leisure and agriculture. Pissarro painted farming villages with a refreshing honesty, his balanced compositions set a documentary modernity in the great Dutch landscape tradition.

As a space located between city and countryside, artifice and nature, modernity and timelessness, the garden was a perfect setting for the impressionist *plein air* project. For example, Renoir's romantic dramas are frequently staged in bourgeois suburban gardens. Claude Monet took the project one stage further and, at his own famous garden at Giverny, carried the colour theories he had developed as a painter through to his planting schemes.

LIST OF PAINTINGS

A Garden of Impressionist Verse
Copyright © Frances Lincoln Ltd 2008
Frances Lincoln Ltd
4 Torriano Mews
Torriano Avenue
London NW5 2RZ
www.franceslincoln.com

British Library Cataloguing in Publication Data available on request
ISBN 978-0-7112-2640-1

IMAGES AND VERSE SELECTED BY MICHAEL BRUNSTROM

Printed and bound by Kwong Fat Offset Printing Co Ltd, Hong Kong
1 3 5 7 9 8 6 4 2